Dis
Mad Libs

D Brooklyn

Mad Libs is fun to play with friends but you can also play it by yourself! To begin with, do not look at the story on the page below. Fill in the blanks on this page with the words called for. Then, using the words you have selected, fill in the blank spaces in the story.

Now you've created your own hilarious Mad Libs game!

[Type here]

Verb -

Noun (plural)-

Adj (most)-

Noun-

Adj-

Noun-

Let's get down to business

To _____ the Huns
      verb

Did they send me _____ when I asked for sons?
                                          Noun

You're the _____ bunch I ever met
                   adj

But you can bet before we're through

Mister, I'll make a _____ out of you
                             noun

_____ as a forest
  adj

But on fire within

Once you find your center

You are sure to win

[Type here]

You're a spineless, pale, pathetic lot

And you haven't got a clue

Somehow I'll make a_____out of you
            noun

Noun-
Noun-
Noun-
Noun (pl)-
Verb-
Noun-
Verb-
Adj-

[Type here]

Oh, imagine a land, it's a faraway place

Where the caravan camels roam

Where you wander among every culture and tongue
It's chaotic, but hey, it's home

When the _____'s from the east
　　　　　　Noun
And the_____'s from the west
　　　　　Noun

And the sand in the glass is right

Come on down, stop on by

Hop a_____ and fly
　　　Noun

To another Arabian night

As you wind through the _____at the fabled bazaars
　　　　　　　　　　　　　　　Noun

With the cardamom-cluttered stalls

You can _____ every spice
       Verb

While you haggle the price

Of the silks and the satin shawls

Oh, the _____that plays
        Noun

As you _____ through a maze
       Verb

In the haze of your _____ delight
                    Adj

You are caught in a dance

You are lost in the trance

Of another Arabian night

[Type here]

Noun-
Noun-
Noun-
Adj-
Adj-

I can show you the _____
  noun
Shining, shimmering, splendid

Tell me, _____
  noun
Now when did you last let your heart decide?

I can open your eyes

Take you wonder by wonder

Over, sideways and under

On a magic _____ ride
  noun

A whole new world

A new fantastic point of view

No one to tell us, "No"

Or where to go

Or say we're only dreaming

[Type here]

A whole new world

A dazzling place I never knew

But when I'm way up here

It's crystal clear

That now I'm in a whole new world with you

Now I'm in a whole new world with you

_____ sights
    adj

_____ feeling
    adj

Soaring, tumbling, freewheeling

Through an endless diamond sky

Noun-

Adj-

Noun (pl)-

Adj-

[Type here]

The _____ is always greener
  Noun

In somebody else's lake

You dream about going up there

But that is a _____ mistake
          Adj

Just look at the _____ around you
              Noun

Right here on the _____ floor
                Adj

Such wonderful things surround you

What more is you lookin' for?

Under the sea

Under the sea

Darling it's better

Down where it's wetter

Take it from me

Adj-

Adj-

Noun-

Adj-

Noun (pl)-

Noun-

Adj-

Adj-

Adj-

Verb-

[Type here]

Little town

It's a _____ village
          Adj

Every day

Like the one before

Little town

Full of _____ people
          adj

Waking up to say

Bonjour bonjour

Bonjour bonjour bonjour

There goes the baker with his _____, like always
                                       noun

The same old bread and rolls to sell

Every morning just the same

Since the morning that we came

To this _____ provincial town
               Adj

Good morning, Belle

Where you off to?

To return this book to Pere Robert, it's about

two _____ in fair Verona
          Noun

Look at her, LeFou

My future _____
             Noun

Belle is the most _____ girl in the village
                        adj

That's makes her the best

But she's so well-read

And you're so athletically-inclined

Yes, ever since the war, I felt like I've been missing something

[Type here]

She's the only girl that ever given me that sense of

Mmm je ne sais quoi?

I don't know what that means

Right from the moment when I met her, saw her

I said she's _____ and I fell
               adj

Here in town there's only she

Who is _____ as me
         adj

So I'm making plans to _____ and marry Belle
                                    verb

Verb (s)-

Noun-

Noun-

Adj-

Adj-

Adj-

Adj-

Noun-

Noun (pl)-

Noun-

Verb-

[Type here]

Gosh, it _____ me to see you Gaston
        verb

Looking so down in the dumps

Every _____ here'd love to be you, Gaston
          Noun

Even when taking your lumps

There's no _____ in town as admired as you
        noun

You're everyone's _____ guy
            Adj

Everyone's awed and inspired by you

And it's not very hard to see why

No one's _____ as Gaston
        Adj

No one's _____ as Gaston
        adj

No one's neck's as incredibly _____ as Gaston's
        adj

For there's no _____ in town half as manly
                  noun

Perfect, a pure paragon

You can ask any Tom, Dick, or Stanley

And they'll tell you whose team they prefer to be on

Who play _____ like Gaston?
              Noun

Who break hearts like Gaston?

Who's much more than the sum of his parts like Gaston?

As a _____ , yes, I'm intimidating
       Noun

My, what a _____, that Gaston!
                Noun

I needed encouragement

Thank you LeFou

Well, there's no one…

[Type here]

Noun-
Noun-
Adj-
Verb-
Adj-
Noun-
Noun-
Adj-

A long time ago in a land far away
Lived the _____ princess Tiki
           noun
She was sweet as a _____ in a pineapple way
                        noun

But so _____ that she hardly speaky
         adj
Still if you _____ well
               verb
you'll hear her _____ wish
                    adj
Aloha, everybody my name is Tiki

I long to free a truly remarkable _____ ,
my sweet prince   Noun

She dreams of a _____ who is under a spell
                     noun

That has left him all _____ and scaly
                          adj
I sing from my heart with the power of love

Just a girl with a ukulele

[Type here]

Noun-

Verb-

Adj-

Noun (pl)-

Verb-

Noun-

Verb-

Verb-

Verb-

Some day my _____ will come
             noun

Some day I'll _____ my love
              verb

And how _____ that moment will be
         adj

When the prince of my _____ comes to me
                       noun

He'll whisper, I love you

And _____ a kiss or two
     verb

Though he's far away

I'll find my _____ some day
              noun

Some day when my dreams come true

Some day I'll _____ my love
              verb

Someone to call my own

And I'll _____ her the moment we meet
          verb

For my heart will start skipping a beat

[Type here]

Some day we'll _____ and do
               verb
Things we've been longing to

Verb-
Noun-
Noun-
Adj-
Verb (-ed)-
Noun-
Adj-

[Type here]

This is what you give me to _____ with
                                    verb

Well, _____, I've seen worse
         noun

We're going to turn this _____'s ear
                                noun

Into a _____ purse
        adj

We'll have you _____ and dried
                     verb

Primped and polished

Till you glow with pride

Trust me recipe for instant bride

You'll bring honor to us all

Wait and see

When we're through

Boys will gladly go to _____ for you
                              noun

With good fortune

And a _____ hairdo
       adj

You'll bring honor to us all

Noun-
Noun-
Noun-
Verb (-ing)-
Verb (-ing)-
Verb (-ing)-
Verb (-ing)-
Verb-
Noun-

[Type here]

There's 104 days of _____ vacation
                            noun
And _____ comes along just to end it
         noun
So the annual _____ for our generation
                     noun
Is _____a good way to spend it
   verb
Like maybe...

_____ a rocket
   verb
Or _____ a mummy
     verb
Or _____ up the Eiffel Tower
     verb
_____ something that doesn't exist (Hey!)
  verb
Or giving a _____ a shower
               noun

Noun-
Noun-
Noun-
Noun (pl)-

[Type here]

"Look at that, Abu! It's not every day you see a _____ with two rear ends."
              noun
- Aladdin

"You know how men are. They think _____ means _____ and 'Get lost'
      Noun   Noun
means 'Take me, I'm yours.'"
- Meg, *Hercules*

"I want to do something for her… but what?"

"Well, there's the usual things: flowers, chocolates, _____ you don't intend to keep…"
                    Noun

- Beast and Cogsworth, *Beauty and the Beast*

Noun-
Noun (an)-
Noun-
Noun-
Verb-

[Type here]

"You are a toy! You aren't the real
_____! You're – you're an _____
          Noun   Noun
figure!
You are a _____'s play thing!"
                     Noun

"You are a sad, strange little _____, and
you have my pity."   Noun
- Woody and Buzz, *Toy Story*

"What do you want me to do, dress in drag and
do the _____?"
              Verb

- Timon, *The Lion King*

Noun (pl)-

Noun-

Noun (pl)-

Noun-

Adj-

Verb-

Noun (pl)-

Noun (pl)-

Verb (-ed)-

[Type here]

Jessie: Buzz! We're your _____!
                          Noun

Buzz Lightyear: Spare me your _____, temptress!
                               Noun

Your emperor's defeated, and I'm immune to your bewitching good looks.

"Aw, poor guy. I understand. It's not easy being banished. Take my buddy Bigfoot. When he was banished, he fashioned an enormous diaper out of _____.
           Noun

Wore it on his head like a _____.
                            Noun

Called himself 'King _____.'"
                      Adj

- Yeti, *Monsters, Inc.*

Sergeant Calhoun: "Fear" is a four-letter word, ladies!
You wanna go _____ in your big-boy slacks,
                     Verb
keep it to yourself!

"I know what the big question is: did Rapunzel and I ever get _____?
                                                                  Noun
Well I'm pleased to tell you that after years and years of asking and asking and asking... I finally said _____."
         Noun
"Eugene..."
"Alright, I _____ her."
                verb

[Type here]

Adj-

Noun-

Noun-

Noun-

Verb-

Noun-

Verb-

Noun-

Verb (-ing)-

Adj-

Cruella De Vil: Anita, darling!

Anita: How are you?
Cruella De Vil: _____, darling, as usual,
                     Adj

perfectly wretched.

"Honey?"
"What?"
"Where's my super suit?"
"What?"
"Where is my super suit?!"
"I, uh, put it away."
"Where?"
"Why do you need to know?"
"I need it!"
"Uh-uh! Don't you think about running off doing no daring-do. We've been planning this dinner for two months!"
"The public is in danger!"
"My _____'s in danger!"
        Noun
"You tell me where my _____ is, woman!
                                   Noun

[Type here]

We are talking about the greater good!"

"'Greater good'? I am your _____!
                                      Noun
I'm the greatest good you are ever gonna get!"
- Frozone and Honey, *The Incredibles*

Elsa: You can't _____ a man you just met.
                       Verb

"I am a nice _____, not a mindless eating
                    Noun
machine. If I am to change this image, I
must first _____ myself.
               Verb
Fish are friends, not food."
- Bruce, *Finding Nemo*

Don: I don't want you to think of me as your new _____. After all, we're fraternity

       Noun

brothers first.

Squishy: This is so weird.

Don: Just think of me as your big brother that's _____ your mother. Wait, hold on, we're

Verb

brothers who share the same mom slash wife.

"But without my voice, how can I…"

"You'll have your looks, your pretty face… and don't underestimate the importance of _____ language."

Adj

- Ariel and Ursula, *The Little Mermaid*

[Type here]

Made in the USA
Monee, IL
03 December 2020